a literary lei

I kupu ke aʻa i ke kumu
I lau a puka ka muʻo
Ka liko, ka ao i luna

That the leaf may grow from the stem
That the young shoot may put forth and leaf
Pushing up the enfolded bud

from a prayer to Laka

a literary lei

flowers & plants of hawai'i

COMPILED, EDITED, AND INTRODUCED BY

Jim & Virginia Wageman

PHOTOGRAPHS BY JIM WAGEMAN

WATERMARK PUBLISHING HONOLULU

The credits on page 128 constitute an extension of this copyright page.

ISBN: 0-9742672-5-2
Library of Congress Control Number: 2004104987

Designed by Jim Wageman, Wigwag

Watermark Publishing
1088 Bishop Street
Honolulu, HI 96813
Telephone: 1-808-587-7766
Toll-free: 1-866-900-BOOK
Web site: www.bookshawaii.net
e-mail: sales@bookshawaii.net

Printed in the Republic of Korea

*for all who cherish the land
and its many gifts
—and for our children
and their children*

Hū wale aʻe nā hoʻomanaʻo ana
No nā aliʻi kaulana.
Ua pau, ua hala lākou,
A koe no nā pua.
Ua pau, ua hala lākou,
A koe no nā pua.

E lei i ka lei haʻaheo o Hawaiʻi,
Ka wehi hoʻi o nā aliʻi i hala.
E paʻa ka manaʻo me ka lōkahi,
E mau ke ea o ka ʻāina i ka pono.

Memories come
Of the famous chiefs.
They are gone, they have passed,
And their flowers survive.
They are gone, they have passed,
And their flowers survive.

Wear the cherished leis of Hawaiʻi,
Adornment of departed chiefs.
May all unite in recalling,
The life of the land is perpetuated
    in righteousness.

lyrics from "Nā Aliʻi" / "The Chiefs"
by Samuel Kuahiwi

contents

flowers and plants and hawai'i

IN OUR CONTEMPORARY WORLD—IN OUR RUSH TO BULLDOZE, develop, pave, and otherwise alter the landscape—it is easy to lose touch altogether with our natural environment, to view it as something to be overcome rather than something of intrinsic value that can nourish both body and soul as no amount of concrete or asphalt will ever do. Technology has enabled us to go about the business of environmental degradation with an awesome—at times alarming—effectiveness, often at the service of a mindset that values short-term personal profit over the legacy we will bequeath to future generations. Such was not always the case, and this little book may serve as a small reminder of the rich physical and spiritual heritage the natural world has bestowed on us.

Plants have always been essential to the world's peoples, not only as basic foodstuffs, sources of medicine, and raw materials from which tools are made and shelters constructed, but as powerful spiritual and symbolic components within many cultures. Since time immemorial, plants have played important roles in the rites and rituals of humankind: in the official ceremonies of government and religion, in celebrations of personal achievement, friendship, and love, in the honoring of life's beginning and of its conclusion. Flowers have been so esteemed that they have been chosen as emblems of regional and political entities. One of many examples is the hibiscus, different varieties of which serve as both state flower of Hawai'i and national flower of South Korea and of Malaysia. In Hawai'i, the many cultures that have come to make the islands their home brought their own plant-related traditions, and the intermingling among ethnic groups has served at times to enrich those traditions.

Red Ginger

Naʻenaʻe

Anyone marveling at the tropical greenery and profusion of floral splendor that are such important parts of Hawai'i's appeal might well fail to ponder the incredible phenomena that brought all this luxuriant growth into being. In the beginning, the islands of Hawai'i's archipelago burst forth as magma spewing from a hot spot deep within the Earth's crust. Over some eighty million years, the tectonic Pacific Plate, on its inexorable west-northwest course, has traversed the spot; and one by one the islands have emerged as volcanoes from the sea, swelling to majestic proportions, then subsiding, ultimately succumbing to the relentlessly destructive forces of wind and water and the cataclysmic upheavals of earthquake and landslide. The Hawaiian islands themselves are but the latest arrivals in this ancient chain. The oldest of today's main islands, Kaua'i, was formed only 5.6 million years ago; the youngest, Hawai'i, less than half a million years ago; the very newest arrival, Lō'ihi, is forming even now, a nascent seamount deep within the ocean to the southeast of the chain.

The islands are part of the most isolated archipelago on Earth. The nearest atolls lie 1,000 miles to the south, while the nearest continent, North America, is over 2,000 miles to the east. All life forms had to survive arduous journeys by water or by wind to reach these distant, desolate shores. Survival, after arrival, generally meant adapting to and evolving within the new environment, but those forms that so succeeded were able to enjoy millenia free from many of the natural enemies commonly found elsewhere in the world. Before the arrival of the Polynesians and the pigs that they introduced, no plant-eating mammals existed in the islands. As plants flourished, the barren volcanic landscape was slowly transformed into one of lush greenery, a process that even today may be witnessed on the island of Hawai'i, where, amid the hardened black lava of recent flows, tender shoots of *'ōhi'a lehua* and tiny ferns find their way into cracks in the surface and begin to take hold.

The first humans to reach these shores seem to have descended from an earlier, largely mysterious culture known as the Lapita. It is generally believed that the Polynesian descendants of the Lapita came from the Marquesas Islands to the south, reaching Hawai'i possibly as early as A.D. 300. These Polynesians brought with them around thirty plant species, including such staples as yams, sweet potatoes, bananas, taro, and breadfruit, as well as other plants they valued, among them gourds, coconuts, sugar cane, ti, and *wauke,* or paper mulberry, from which they made tapa. They found here some two thousand plant species, including well over a thousand species of flowering plants, more than ninety percent of them endemic.

The importance that plants played in the spiritual traditions of the Hawaiians may be seen in one of their legends, one version of which tells of the union of Wākea, Sky Father, and Ho'ohōkūkalani. Their stillborn first child, a boy, was buried at night, and by the next morning a taro plant had emerged from his grave. Wākea's second son, Hāloa, the ancestor of the Hawaiian people, was named after that plant. The name Hāloa in fact means "long stalk." King Kalākaua, who claimed descent from Hāloa, incorporated the taro leaf symbol in his crown. Taro was also considered an embodiment, or *kino lau,* of Kāne, chief among the four major gods, the source of water and giver of life.

Taro

Sugar Cane

One of the rites of passage every Hawaiian boy went through, whether child of the *ali'i* (chiefs) or of the *maka'āinana* (commoners), included a dedication to Lono, god of planting, fertility, rain, and harvests. Perhaps more than any other Polynesians, the Hawaiians were industrious and knowledgeable planters and cultivators of the land. Their perceptive observations regarding all plants, both cultivated and wild, resulted in an extensive system of naming and classification.

The Europeans and Americans who began to arrive in the late 18th and early 19th centuries soon began to exploit the land commercially. By mid-19th century, sugar plantations were in need of laborers from abroad. Those who came to work on the plantations—Chinese, Japanese, Filipinos, and others—ultimately emerged as important ethnic groups in Hawai'i's increasingly cosmopolitan cultural fabric. The profound appreciation that these groups felt for the ameliorative power of plants is suggested by a Chinese proverb: "When you have only two pennies left in the world, buy a loaf of bread with one and a lily with the other."

Since antiquity, plants have been integral to Asian cultural and religious observances. In ancient China sansevierias were brought into homes, monasteries, and places of work so that through them the Eight Gods might transmit the eight virtues, among them prosperity, intelligence, good health, strength, and long life. For the Japanese, even today, the *kadomatsu,* a New Year's decoration assembled from bamboo, pine boughs, and plum-tree sprigs, represents a similar source of beneficence, the bamboo signifying strength and prosperity, the pine boughs longevity, and the plum-tree sprigs constancy. The traditional Japanese art of *ikebana,* or flower arranging, which in Hawai'i has been adapted to take advantage of such tropical flowers as birds-of-paradise and plumerias, evolved from the spiritual beliefs of Buddhism, particularly Zen. The narcissus, for the Chinese, and the cherry blossom, for the Japanese, symbolize virtue and beauty, among other concepts, and are today the emblems of annual festivals held to select and honor young women personifying such ideals. The Filipinos share a heritage of flowers as a part of such traditional celebrations as the Flores de Mayo festival, in which they are gathered to decorate parish churches, honor the Virgin Mary, and welcome the rains that will nourish the new crops. The lotus—upon which, in some traditions, the Buddha himself was born—has long been esteemed among Chinese, Japanese, Koreans, Thais, Indians, and other Asians, especially Buddhists and Hindus. It is revered as a symbol of fertility and prosperity and of beauty emerging from the murkiest and muddiest of depths—virtue and spiritual liberation successfully surmounting defilement and sin.

Such is the power that plants have held over the imagination, the stimulus they have provided to our spiritual and our metaphysical lives.

The pages that follow offer a sampling of excerpts from writings that touch directly or indirectly on some of the many flowers and plants that are a part of Hawai‘i's bountiful landscape. The selection is intentionally broad, ranging from the sublime poetry of the Kumulipo to the not infrequently ridiculous lyrics of *hapa haole* hula songs, the whole a tribute to the many and diverse peoples who have contributed to the cultural and botanical richness that is Hawai‘i's.

The lei is a garland of love, a gesture of aloha. Herewith, a literary lei.

a literary lei

O kalina a ka wai i hoʻoulu ai
O ka huli hoʻokawowo honua
O paia [ʻa] i ke auau ka manawa
O heʻe au loloa ka po
O piha, o pihapiha
O piha-u, o piha-a
O piha-e, o piha-o
O ke koʻo honua paʻa ka lani
O lewa ke au, ia Kumulipo ka po
     Po-no

Water . . . causes the withered vine to flourish
Causes the plant top to develop freely
Multiplying in the passing time
The long night slips along
Fruitful, very fruitful
Spreading here, spreading there
Spreading this way, spreading that way
Propping up earth, holding up the sky
The time passes, this night of Kumulipo
    Still it is night

from *The Kumulipo:*
A Hawaiian Creation Chant

ʻIeʻie

The Hawaiians twined
fine baskets and fish
traps from the aerial
roots of the endemic
ʻieʻie vine. They used
those roots as well
to fashion basketry
substructures to which
colorful feathers were
attached for the helmets
worn in battle by the
aliʻi, or chiefs. The
ʻieʻie, itself considered
sacred, also served to
represent a deity on the
altar of the hula hālau,
or instruction hall, a
consecrated structure.

I luna la, i luna
Nā manu o ka lewa

I lalo la, i lalo
Nā pua o ka honua

I uka la, i uka
Nā ulu lāʻau

I kai la, i kai
Nā iʻa o ka moana

Haʻina mai ka puana
A he nani ke ao nei

Above, above
all birds in air

Below, below
all earth's flowers

Inland, inland
all forest trees

Seaward, seaward
all ocean fish

Sing out and say
again the refrain

Behold this lovely world

"Eʻlke Mai" / "Behold"
chant composed by Mary Kawena Pukui

Spiral Ginger

*This little spiral ginger
is known more formally
as* Costus barbatus.
*Blooming ginger plants
are related to the gingers
from whose roots the
spice derives. In
Hawaiʻi, ginger
has many medicinal
purposes. Juices
from the flowers are
used in shampoos,
and the roots and
leaves have healing
qualities. Ginger
tea is a favorite
cure-all.*

Aloha Oʻahu lei ka ʻilima
Kohu manu ʻōʻō hulu melemele

Beloved is Oʻahu with the ʻilima lei
Like the ʻōʻō birds its golden plumage

lyrics from "Aloha Oʻahu"
by Clarence Kinney

28

ʻIlima

The ʻilima, related
to the hibiscus, is found
in several varieties.
The one shown here is
the official flower of
the island of Oʻahu and
was once quite popular
for making leis. The
Hawaiians used the
ʻilima's flowers and its
roots medicinally. They
also considered it to be
one of the forms that
the goddess Laka
could assume.

I lie dreaming
when my father comes to me and says,
I hope you write a book someday.
He thinks I waste my time,
but outside, he spends hours over stones,
gauging the size and shape a rock will take
to fill a space,
to make a wall of dreams around our home.
In the house he built with his own hands
I wish for the lure that catches all fish
or girls with hair like long moss in the river.
His thoughts are just as far and old
as the lava chips like flint off the hammer,
and he sees the mold of dreams
taking shape in his hands.
His eyes see across orchids on the wall,
into black rock, down to the sea,
and he remembers the harbor full of fish,
orchids in the hair of women thirty years before
he thought of me, this home, these stone walls.
Some rocks fit perfectly, slipping into place
with light taps of his hammer.
He thinks of me inside
and takes a big slice of stone,
and pounds it into the ground
to make the corner of the wall.
I cannot wake until I bring
the fish and the girl home.

"Poem for My Father" by Eric Chock

Orchid

Sultry and infused
with glamour, no flower
suggests the tropics more
than the orchid, over
700 varieties of which
grow in Hawai'i. Wild
orchids can be spotted
along woodland trails;
others are propagated in
nurseries and by orchid
enthusiasts. The Vanda,
pictured here, has a
pleasing fragrance,
though many orchids
are not scented. Most
orchids are epiphytes, or
air plants, and need no
soil in which to grow.
Many trees in Hawai'i
are host to gorgeous
blooming orchids.

Ka poʻe kahiko *[the people of old] were
familiar with the god in the thunder.
Sometimes he appeared in human form . . .
but without changing his character as
an "angel," to associate with men and to
speak to them in visions and trances. . . .
At other times he showed his supernatural
form . . . which was like that of a man,
with his feet on the earth and his head
in space among the rolling clouds. The
right side of his body, the god side, was
a very deep black from head to foot, and
the left side, white from head to foot. . . .
That was Kanehekili's "angel" body in
a man; his body as a god . . . which no
man has ever seen, is the thunder. . . .*

   *From the very beginning Kanehekili
appeared with one side a deep black.
This is the reason why Kahekili, the ruler
of Maui, was tattooed a solid black . . .
from head to foot on the right side.
His whole company of warrior chiefs . . .
and household companions . . . were
tattooed in the same way. . . .*

from *Ka Poʻe Kahiko: The People of Old*
by Samuel Manaiakalani Kamakau

ʻIlieʻe

*The Hawaiians
used the leaves of this
indigenous wildflower,
a type of plumbago,
to treat sprains. Taken
internally, however,
it is poisonous. Its
sap was used to
blacken tattoos.*

I go by the trail
of earth and green
slivers of sun
pendulous rain.

I go by the dream trees
flame trees hissing
and swaying.

I go by the shores
and coconut dunes, soft crab
sand in my heart.

I go by the temples
maile vines fresh
with tears.

I go by the taro
velvet-leafed god
flesh and mud.

I go by the thrust
of Kōnāhuanui
his lava jet
jewelled with fern.

I go by the moons
expectant
feeling in the throat
for the chanter.

"I Go by the Moons"
by Haunani-Kay Trask

34

Maile

For the early
Hawaiians, maile
was sacred to Laka,
goddess of the hula,
and was one of the five
plants placed on the
altar of the hula hālau.
The vinelike shrub is
found in a variety of
forms, with varying
leaf shapes, growing
wild on most of the
islands. Its fragrant
leaves make maile as
popular today as in
ancient times for use in
leis or other decorative
adornment. The maile
commonly used for leis
has oval-shaped leaves,
one to three inches
long—smaller and
more pointed than
those of the type shown
here, which is one of
several native plants
that may be found
on the grounds of
Kawaiaha'o Church,
in Honolulu.

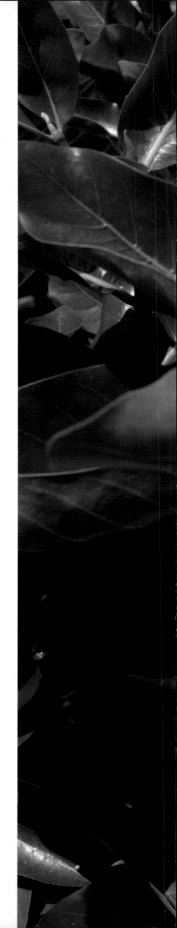

E ka gentle breeze a pā mai nei
Hoʻohāliʻaliʻa mai ana iaʻu
E kuʻu sweet never-fading flower
I pua i ka uka o Paoakalani

O gentle breeze that wafts to me
Sweet, cherished memories of you
Of my sweet never-fading flower
That blooms in the fields of Paoakalani

lyrics from "Kuʻu Pua I Paoakalani"
by Queen Liliʻuokalani

Protea

*The upcountry area
of East Maui provides
growing conditions
highly favorable to the
cultivation of protea,
plants whose origins are
in South Africa. There,
on Maui, these colorful
and exotic blooms are
propagated at the
University of Hawaiʻi's
experimental farm, and
they are also grown
commercially. The
flowers may still be
enjoyed long after
they have dried.*

Ku'u wahine e—e hoi mai kāua.
Aia la o ka nahele o Kūmanomano
Ke hehia mai la e ka la o Kamakali'i,
Ke kakali la ia Kaelo me Ikiiki,
Na huhui 'awa a Makali'i e.

O my love, come back to me!
The thick groves at Kūmanomano
Are being trampled by the summer sun;
It lingers for the sun of Kaelo and Ikiiki,
And for the bunches of 'awa of Makali'i.

from "Legend of Halemano"

'Awa

*This shrub, a member
of the black pepper
family, is the source
of a mildly narcotic
concoction made from
the masticated roots
mixed with water and
drunk as a relaxant.
For the Hawaiians, the
root and drink were also
important components
of religious ceremonies
in which they were used
as solemn offerings to the
gods. Nineteenth-century
Hawaiian historian
Samuel M. Kamakau
relates that at the time
"when the gods mingled
with men," the "tabus
and laws of the chiefs
[and] the tabus of the
gods" were handed
down "over the 'awa
cup." Medicinal uses
included the treatment
of headaches by
placing 'awa leaves
on the forehead.*

*My father was a laborer from Korea and
my mother was his picture bride. Their lives
crossed many paths between the Waianae
and Koolau mountains of Oahu. I have
seen the places their feet walked over, bodies
arched to the ground, planting pineapple
slips. And when the plants matured, they
stooped over and over a million more times
to pick ripened fruit, filling pineapple crates,
then loading heavy crates onto trucks that
went to the cannery. At the end of each day,
workers returned to their plantation homes
or to their homes in Wahiawa.*

*I am the last born in my family and did
not work the fields. But I remember being six
years old, the noise of trucks taking men and
women laborers out to the pineapple fields
as I crossed the bridge to go to school. . . .*

from "A Place of Noise" by Daisy Chun Rhodes

Pineapple

*Pineapple was first
grown commercially in
Hawai'i in the late 19th
century as a supplement
to the sugar industry,
but by the early 1930s
the pineapple industry
was thriving in its own
right, filling orders for
three-quarters of the
world's market. As with
sugar, however, by the
close of the 20th century
Hawai'i's pineapple
industry, overtaken by
foreign competition, had
declined considerably.*

The night air at Honolulu airport was . . .
warm and velvety, almost palpable. To feel
it on your face was like being licked by a
large friendly dog, whose breath smelled
of frangipani . . . and you felt it almost
instantly on arrival, because the walkways—
stuffy glazed corridors in most airports, mere
extensions of the claustrophobic aircraft cabin—
were here open at their sides to the air. He and
his father were soon sweating again in their
thick English clothes, but a light breeze fanned
their cheeks and rustled in the floodlit palm
trees. A kind of tropical garden had been
laid out next to the terminal building, with
artificial ponds and streams, and naked torches
burning amid the foliage. It was this spectacle
which seemed to convince Mr Walsh that
they had finally arrived at their destination.
He stopped and gawped. "Look at that,"
he said. "Jungle."

from *Paradise News, A Novel* by David Lodge

Plumeria

Plumeria trees provide
blossoms for thousands
of leis made daily in
Hawai'i. Known in
other parts of the world
as frangipani, the
plumeria has delicately
scented flowers that are
usually white, pink,
yellow, or orange. Many
plumeria trees lose their
blossoms and leaves
during several months
of the year, the skeletons
of their limbs forming
elegant patterns
against the sky.

The god Kū . . . once came to Hawai'i and married a Hawaiian woman, with whom he lived many years and raised a large family. He did not tell the woman that he was a god; he worked on the land like anybody else.

A time came when food was scarce. . . . Kū's wife and children were starving. Kū was sorry for them. He told his wife that he could get food for them by going on a long journey but that he could never return. . . . At first, his wife would not hear of it, but she finally consented to his going. . . . Kū said, "Let us go into the yard." There he said good-bye to the woman and told her that he was going to stand on his head and disappear into the earth. Then she must wait until his toes appeared out of the ground. Out of them would grow food for the family. He stood on his head and began to sink into the ground; first his head and shoulders, then finally his whole body disappeared.

His wife watched the spot every day and watered it with her tears. One day a sprout appeared, and from it a tree grew so rapidly that in a few days the family had the food that Kū had promised. It was the breadfruit.

from "The Breadfruit Tree"

44

Breadfruit

This glorious tree, 'ulu in Hawaiian, was introduced to the islands by the early Polynesian settlers, who used its light wood for surfboards and canoes and its sap as caulk for the canoes. The starchy fruit was steamed and pounded before eating as breadfruit poi.

The further I traveled through the town [Honolulu] the better I liked it. Every step revealed a new contrast— disclosed something I was unaccustomed to. . . . [I]n place of the customary geranium, calla lily, etc., languishing in dust and general debility, I saw luxurious banks and thickets of flowers, fresh as a meadow after a rain, and glowing with the richest dyes. . . .

from *Roughing It in the Sandwich Islands*
by Mark Twain

Parrot's Beak

This charming and colorful plant, a native of tropical America, may be the most commonly found heliconia in the islands. It blooms year round, providing a cheerful accent to any garden graced by its presence. Like all heliconias, it is an herb related to the banana.

There was an autumn chill without the autumn colors. We wore layers of clothes
and haori *jackets or shawls and walked with unhurried grace. The garden felt*
summery with poincianas, geraniums, red ginger, willows, and gardenia. Skylarks
hovered overhead, trilling their birdsongs. Rainbows arced across the makai *sky.*
San-O-samas hillock was an anthill compared to Haleakala, which gave birth
to the sun each morning. In the afternoon the fog would creep down the massive
slope and shroud the bean-sized cattle, trees, and cacti.

from *Five Years on a Rock* by Milton Murayama

Na'ena'e

Na'ena'e's *scientific*
name is dubautia. *It is*
an endemic Hawaiian
shrub related to the
silversword. The species
pictured here, Dubautia
menziesii, *photographed*
in Haleakalā crater, is
found only at higher
altitudes on East Maui.
Like the silverswords,
dubautias *are members*
of the daisy family. The
Hawaiian name also
came to mean "fragrant,"
for the sweetness of the
na'ena'e's *blossoms.*

*Every hibiscus in Hawaii, no matter
what other kind of hibiscus it's crossed
with, its color, or its size, is the official
Flower of Hawaii. This all came about
in 1923 when the legislature proclaimed
it to be Hawaii's official flower, "no other
flower having so great a variety in color
and form or such continuous blooming."
Also, very few other flowers are as hardy,
or have as cosmopolitan an appearance.
Just like Hawaii's people.*

from "The Hibiscus" by Genie Pitchford

Hibiscus

*As Pitchford observed
(see above), in 1923 the
Territorial legislature
named the hibiscus, in
all its varieties, the
official flower of the
Islands. In 1988—nearly
thirty years after Hawai'i
was admitted to the
Union—the endemic
and endangered all-
yellow* ma'o hau hele
(H. brackenridgei), *
shown opposite, was
designated the state's
official flower.*

Mai Puna hoʻi au i hele mai nei,
Ua ʻike mai nei hoʻi au i nā wahine kōhi noni,
Waʻuwaʻu noni,
Pākuikui noni,
Kākau noni. . . .

It is from Puna that I have come
And I have seen the women gathering noni,
Scratching noni,
Pounding noni,
Marking with noni. . . .

from "Tradition of Kamapuaa"

Noni

The early Polynesian settlers brought noni, *or Indian mulberry, to Hawaiʻi. A native of Asia and of other Pacific islands,* noni *is an evergreen plant belonging to the coffee family. The Hawaiians extracted dyes from it and used it medicinally as well. Its potential as the source of a possible cancer-fighting agent is today the subject of ongoing research.*

Lele ana Ka-ʻena me he manu ala,
I ka mālie me he kahaʻana nā ke kaʻupu
Ke one o Nēnē-lēʻa,
Me he upaʻi ala nā koaʻe
I waho la o ka ʻale o Ka-ʻieʻie.

Ka-ʻena reaches out like a bird flying overhead,
a sea-gannet soaring in a still sky
above sandy Nēnē-lēʻa,
a bo'sunbird high over the channel of Ka-ʻieʻie—
a flapping of wings.

from "Hiʻi-aka's Song at Ka-ʻena"

54

Pāʻū-o-Hiʻiaka

Related to the morning glory, this native vine may be found clinging to the sand along island shores. Kaʻena Point, on Oʻahu, was home to the one shown here and to the albatross soaring overhead. The flowers may be white or pale blue. The name means "skirt of Hiʻiaka" and derives from a myth in which the volcano goddess, Pele, left her baby sister, Hiʻiaka, on the beach while going off to fish. Upon her return, Pele found that the vine had formed a skirt to protect the infant from the sun. The song excerpted here was sung, in legend, by an older Hiʻiaka on her way to Kauaʻi to bring back Pele's desired lover, Lohiʻau.

As we mounted the glacis of the island, the horses clattering on the lava, we saw far above us the curtain of the rain exclude the view. The sky was clear, the sun strong overhead; around us a thin growth of bushes and creepers glittered green in their black setting, like plants upon a ruinous pavement; all else was lava, wastes of lava. . . . But the bushes, when the rain descends often enough from its residential altitude, flourish extremely. . . .

from *Travels in Hawaii* by Robert Louis Stevenson

‘Ōhai

A native Hawaiian shrub that is now rare and endangered, ‘ōhai once grew abundantly in such areas as Ka‘ena Point on the island of O‘ahu. It may still be found on most of the islands, though mainly in just a few remote coastal areas.

The yellow alamanda sprawls
In gold confusion on the walls
And in among its flower-suns
The little starry jasmine runs.
The bougainvillea climbs the trees
And flings its tatters on the breeze
All scarlet and magenta-red . . .
A canopy above my head.

from "My Hawaiian Garden"
by Don Blanding

Allamanda

A climbing shrub
native to Brazil, the
allamanda is closely
related to the plumeria
as well as to the natal
plum that is commonly
used as a hedge in the
islands. Its lovely
flowers—their radiant
yellow an echo of one of
the colors of Hawaiian
royalty—were quite
possibly the inspiration
for the plant's name in
Hawaiian, lani ali'i,
or "heavenly chief." A
variant double form
is shown at left.

*In the deep shade of this perennial greenery the
people dwell. . . . The peculiarity in which all
seem to share is, that everything is decorated and
festooned with flowering trailers. It is often
difficult to tell what the architecture is, or what
is house and what is vegetation; for all angles,
and lattices, and balustrades, and verandahs are
hidden by jessamine or passion-flowers, or the
gorgeous flamelike Bougainvilliers. . . . Each
house has a large garden or "yard," with lawns
of bright perennial greens and banks of blazing,
many-tinted flowers, and lines of Dracaena, and
other foliage plants, with their great purple or
crimson leaves, and clumps of marvellous lilies,
gladiolas, ginger, and many plants unknown to
me. Fences and walls are altogether buried by
passion-flowers, the night-blowing Cereus, and
the tropaeolum, mixed with geraniums, fuschia,
and jessamine, which cluster and entangle over
them in indescribable profusion. A soft air moves
through the upper branches, and the drip of
water from miniature fountains falls musically
on the perfumed air.*

from *Six Months in the Sandwich Islands* by Isabella Bird

Monstera

*Like taro, monstera
is a member of the
arum family, which
includes anthurium,
spathiphyllum, calla
lilies, philodendron,
and many others. Of
some thirty monstera
species, all originating
in tropical America,
one (M. deliciosa) is
commonly found in
Hawai'i. Its conical
fruit is edible, with
a taste resembling
a blend of banana
and pineapple.*

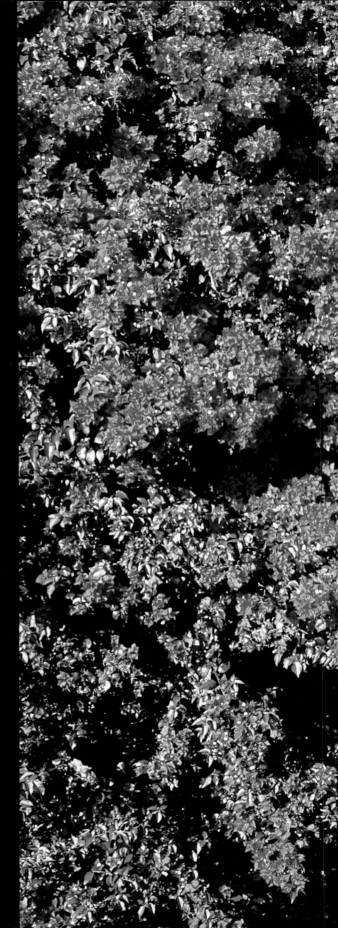

My father and three Tongans
built this wall . . . .
And the bougainvillea they
   transplanted
from a seedling has grown
extravagant with age,
spilling a waterfall of blossoms,
purple and fuchsia.
I see the matchstick house,
riddled with termites,
had a luxuriance
my brother and I imagined.
But the sense of refuge was real.

from "Shadow Figures"
by Cathy Song

Bougainvillea

Bougainvillea are
named in honor of the
famous 18th-century
French navigator Louis
A. de Bougainville, who
first encountered them
at Rio de Janeiro,
Brazil. Large, woody
vines, they are often
cultivated to form
spectacularly
colorful hedges.

This morning Wick and I drove up
to Tantalus to pick white ginger for
Annabel's lei. . . .
    He liked the winding road, wanted
to take it all the way up and then back
down Round Top Drive. . . . He couldn't
believe how beautiful it was up there.
Like what he expected Hawaii to be.
Lush and tropical. Not so many houses
and cars and hotels. Exotic. Exotic.
He said it twice.

   .   .   .   .   .   .

    We picked enough ginger for two
leis. I sewed one. He sewed one.
    He said, This is my first lei! My
very first! Wait till Beet sees this.
Do you think she'll like it?
    His lei was very sad, the flowers
all brown where he squeezed too hard.
His father, Coy, would be so proud.

from *Makai* by Kathleen Tyau

White Ginger

Many species of ginger
are found throughout
the Hawaiian islands.
The white ginger species
is especially fragrant and
is extremely popular for
making leis. Perfume
is also commercially
produced from
its flowers.

Wehiwehi nei pua naʻu e kui
Ke kipona ʻia me ka maʻo
A he pua kapu ʻia na ka manu
Na ka ʻiʻiwi pōlena o ka uka

Kaulana e ka ua i Waʻahila
I ka hehi i ke ono o ke pili
Hoʻokahi no ʻoe o laila
Me ka rain Tuahine o Mānoa

These flowers I'll string as an adornment
Combined with the maʻo
A blossom sacred to the birds
The honeycreeper of the uplands

Famous is the rain at Waʻahila
Falling upon the pili grass
You are the only one there
With the Tuahine rain of Mānoa

"Rain Tuahine o Mānoa" by Julia Walanika

Maʻo

Also known as
Hawaiian cotton,
maʻo is a native shrub
that grows mainly in
coastal areas. The pods
contain seeds wrapped
in cotton fibers. The
leaves provided a dye of
a fugitive pale green;
from its flowers the
Hawaiians extracted
a yellow dye as well,
which they used in
making tapa.

When my father was alive . . . his garden seemed constantly in bloom. Orchids flowered, acerola cherries multiplied, ti leaves glistened. . . . No matter what the weather . . . when he returned home from work each evening, he would immediately unravel the water hose and for the next hour, standing in white undershirt and navy-blue work pants, he would shower each plant. . . .

First he watered the terraces to the right of the stairs—a jumble of palm, jade plant, Angel's Trumpet, pīkake, dryland taro, lemon grass, and about thirty other varieties of plants. Then he would water the terraces to the left, including the spreading branches of the plumeria tree, the crotons under them, and the bittermelon vines growing wild around the base of the tree's trunk. Next he would turn to the small oval of lawn and the acerola tree that shaded it. The steps to the lower part of the house . . . led down to a row of long-stalked ti, an orange tree, a coconut tree, several banana trees, a patch of heliconia, and an assortment of tropical plants. Back up the other side of the house were his coffee tree, more ti, and a papaya tree. . . .

My father, who was otherwise a talkative and often angry man, always retreated into thoughtful silence while he was watering the garden, as if he too were experiencing a cleansing from all the day's cares and discords, as if he too were being nourished.

from "My Father's Garden" by D. Māhealani Dudoit

Lobster Claw

Lobster claw is one of the most common of the heliconias found in Hawai'i. The plants may grow to a height of six feet, their tiny flowers hidden within the colorful bracts that grow alternately along the stems. The vibrant coloring of the bracts has made the lobster claw a highly popular ornamental. It will last for several weeks after being cut.

This is the story about the poi of my family at Kapaʻahu. Poi is the staff of life of the Hawaiian people. Our type of taro was dry-land taro. It was planted in the mountains because there's more rain there in the mountains and it's damp. And also the other plants were planted there, like sugar-cane, banana, onion, those kinds of things.

From the planting of the taro to the "pulling" (harvesting) is about seven months, and with some kinds of taro about one year. It depends on the type. There're lots of kinds.

And the same with the kind of poi, it depends on the type of taro. Some poi is kind of grey and some poi is kind of darkish. And as for lehua taro, its poi is kind of reddish, kind of pink. However, the various kinds of poi are all equally good-tasting.

from *Story of Kapaʻahu: He Moʻolelo no Kapaʻahu*
by Emma Kapūohuʻulaokalani Kauhi

Taro

To the ancient Hawaiians, taro, or kalo, *was one of the bodies of Kāne, chief among their four major gods. The Polynesians introduced taro to the islands. Only the men were allowed to handle it from cultivation to preparation for eating, although it was then eaten by all. It was in fact the mainstay of the Hawaiians' diet, mainly in the form of poi, made by mashing the cooked corms and mixing them with a little water. The leaves, or* lūʻau—*from which the name of the popular feast derives—are also eaten.*

Me, one emotional illiterate! Flowers fo' my wife? How silly! They wither. I always bought her practical things: dish water, vacuum cleaner, clothes dryer . . . li'dat.

And then, my new awareness! I became flower conscious. The grand art of nature! What caught my eyes the hibiscus, the native flower of our isles, with its vivid colors. The hybrids . . . some solid, some bicolored, the singles, the doubles. Need I mention how I gathered the many scions that I have grafted on my stalk plants? Wat you t'ink I carry a knife fo?

from *Who da Guy?* by Yutaka Kawajo

Hibiscus Hybrid

The hibiscus is often seen tucked behind the ear of a dancer or a kamaʻāina *woman. The Hawaiian name for hibiscus is* aloalo. *There are up to a thousand species in Hawaiʻi. The Holland, pictured here, is a recent hybrid. Only ten species are endemic to Hawaiʻi, the most common being the white hibiscus native to Molokaʻi and Oʻahu (see pages 4–5). Although once nearly extinct, the white hibiscus is making a comeback as nurseries propagate plants and as interest in native Hawaiian culture continues to grow.*

*Just before the clouds covered her kind
face again, she [Mahina, the moon]
revealed to me a gift from the greatest gods:
there, growing out of the earth beside the
path, was a whole clump of* kī *plants.
Swiftly I reached out and pulled from
their stalk a handful of the long cool leaves.
According to custom I should have tucked
one of these leaves into my trousers, to
protect the sacred organs of generation
wherein lies my* mana *and that of my
line. But I did not have time to follow the
ancient law, and I hoped that Kāne would
not mind if I thrust the leaf under the bosom
of my shirt. From other leaves I fashioned
wreaths to place around my wrists, forehead,
and shoulders. The last two leaves I tied
together, to make a* lei *for the horse. With
such protection, the evil spirits, the demons
in mud and water, those malicious beings
from the other world who bring accident
and sickness and sudden death, could not
touch me or cause me harm. Nor could the
great gods punish me for being a proudful
traveler when I bore the amulets which
asked their favor. Ahh, it is a good thing
for a man to have about him the things of
old, to give him comfort in times of jeopardy.*

from *Ka'a'awa: A Novel about Hawai'i in the 1850s*
by O. A. Bushnell

Ti

*In ancient Hawai'i,
ti, or* kī, *was a symbol of
divine power, thought to
provide protection from
psychic evil. Introduced
by the Polynesians, it was
one of the plants placed
as offerings on the altar
of the hula* hālau. *In
everyday applications the
leaves were used to serve
or wrap food, thatch
shelters, and make hula
skirts, raincoats, and
footwear. The under-
ground portion of the
stems was steamed to
extract the sugar, used to
make candy or a liquor.
Shown opposite is a
more recent variety
called Black Magic.*

Deep as lapis, upon their green stems
Flower these glimmering flames of ginger.
Our gaze keeps swimming in,
Allured to the quiet place where blue lies pooled.
Dark leaves. Whorled dark flowers.
As if we were staring at candles,
We fall silent, turning to blue flowers.

How slowly they open into the glowing mind!
They shine doubled, as if already
Remembered. The shock of peace.
The shade of our lost lives burns into bloom.
And returns to us, trembling with immanence.
What can we be sure of, lifted to the soft edge
Of vision? Only the blue fire,
Like ginger, blossoming.

"Blue Ginger: Déjà Vu" —For Harriet Gay on her birthday
by Phyllis Hoge Thompson

Blue Ginger

Native to Brazil, blue
ginger is not a true
ginger but rather a
spiderwort, part of the
family that includes
wandering Jew and
the tradescantias. Its
blossoms as well are not
really blue but a deeply
saturated purple. The
plant spreads by means
of an underground
rhizome, in a manner
similar to bamboo.

. . . so from the fronds floating in
        on the waves the ferns were formed that woke on the mountain
after the night ran through the narrows of changing
        in the darkness without eyes and some were born in the sea
some in fresh water or on land so in the caves were born
        the crickets of each cave ground crickets and when there were trees
tree crickets swordtail crickets and the sound they made
        that in time would be called singing ran through the mountain
born only there were flowering trees and lobelias
        and birds that discovered them and were changed when they tasted them
born was the plover into flight born were the birds
        each from the wingbeats of the others born were the guardians
the noddy at sea guarded by the owl on the mountain
        birds passed the peak in high streams that blacked out the sun
and at daybreak the wet hollows of the earth opened wings
        and flew up in answer into the light and the infant
shoots of the taro uncurled and reached for the morning

from *The Folding Cliffs: A Narrative* by W. S. Merwin

Fern

Ferns played essential
roles in early Hawaiian
culture as food, medicine,
decoration, and adornment.
Ceremonially, a native fern,
the palapalai, *was placed on
the altar of the hula* hālau,
*representing Hiʻiaka, one of
the patron goddesses
of the hula.*

Not only color but form is extraordinary.
The gold-filled night-blooming cereus,
the odd-shaped birds of paradise, the
anthuriums with their brilliant red
patent-leather finish, the bilbergias,
out of the leaf spathe of which comes
an almost unbelievable flower—the
only word for Hawaiian florescence is
extravagant. Nothing as serious as a
league of nations convocation will do
for comparison; perhaps a fashion show,
in which all the impressionist designers
vie with one another to create the
richest dresses on the most outrageously
exhibitionist models, is nearer the mark.

from *Calabashes and Kings: An Introduction*
to Hawaii by Stanley D. Porteus

Bird-of-Paradise

Surely one of the most
exotic of tropical plants,
the bird-of-paradise is
a native of South Africa.
Its distinctive, joyfully
exuberant appearance
has made it a favorite
ornamental for many of
Hawai'i's gardeners as
well as a striking choice
for floral bouquets.

Throughout my childhood, the sugarcane fields most symbolized Hawai'i. It was no surprise then that I based my concept of the local literary community on the idea of a neglected cane field. A "cane field" because many early stories were set in the plantation, and readers still identify local literature as stories of the plantation. I believe it is "neglected" because . . . outside of the literary community, the world takes little notice of our literary activities. . . . I saw each writer as a cane stalk setting down roots; absorbing the sun, the soil, and the spirit of Hawai'i; and sending out leaves in which one could read the patterns of Hawai'i. The established writers were the mature cane of a previous season rooted in the islands' history. My generation's writers were shoots barely out of the ground, finding our place among our elders, looking for a place to flourish.

. . . .

The cane stalks of established literary writers towered above, and rising to meet them, as their stories were published, were my peers. . . . But I saw no place for me—that was fine—I was determined to carve out a place for my work and myself. . . . However long it would take, I would change the definition of "local literature." I was no longer cane, I am a cane spider. I am of the local literary community but am not truly part of it. I nestle in among the stalks, creating a place for myself. No matter how long I will be in the field, I will never again be mistaken for cane.

from "Spiders in the Field: A Young Filipino Writer in Hawai'i"
by Normie Salvador

Sugar Cane

Sugar cane, or kō in Hawaiian, is one of the plants that the Polynesians brought with them to Hawai'i. They associated the plant with Kāne, one of the four major gods. During the early 19th century, a few Chinese immigrants began operating one-man sugar plantations and mills on Hawai'i's outer islands. By the late 19th century and for nearly the entire first half of the 20th, sugar, along with its related industries, was the chief engine driving Hawai'i's economy. Its importance eventually declined with the advent of increased competition from foreign growers.

The Hawaiians had many ways of fishing.
They did pole fishing, which was done
by standing in the ocean close to shore.
They also used throw nets, surrounding
nets, trolling and trap fishing. Early
Hawaiians used bone hooks; and in later
years metal hooks were used and reshaped
to catch certain kinds of fish.

　　The Akia plant was used to stupefy fish.
The bark, roots and leaves were pounded
and placed in a piece of coconut fibre,
and lowered into salt water pools to help
catch fish by temporarily paralyzing them.
They were then placed in cool salt water
to remove the narcotic effect, before they
were eaten.

from *True Stories of the Island of Lanai*
by Lawrence Kainoahou Gay

ʻĀkia

The native ʻākia
belongs to the small
ʻākia family comprised of
herbs, trees, and shrubs
from the subtropics.
The early Hawaiians
used its bark as a source
of fiber and the colorful
orange and gold ʻākia
berries for seed leis.
A toxin from the plant
was also used to stun
and catch fish, as
described in the
passage above.

Oh, come away with me, my sweet
To the isles of happiness complete
Where flow'ring trees are calling you,
Oh, come let us sail on the deep blue sea
Where we'll dream dreams on the great unknown
In a world all our own

lyrics from "Hawaii (Isles of Happiness)"
by Frances H. Gerber and Charles E. King

Goethea

An evergreen shrub
introduced to Hawai'i
from Brazil, goethea
may be found in shady,
forested areas. It belongs
to the hibiscus family
(malvaceae), *whose*
members also include
the flowering maple,
hollyhocks, Turk's cap,
and Hawai'i's 'ilima,
ma'o, *and* milo.

Six months the long green cactus branches sprawl
Like spiny serpents carved from opaque jade,
Gorging themselves with sunlight on the wall
Or seeking dewy coolness in the shade.

Half of a year's white moons yield pallid light;
Dews of a hundred mornings keep them fresh;
Mists cool their sun-parched skin throughout the night;
Earth with volcanic ashes feeds their flesh.

Then on some mystic night . . . who gives the hour . . .
Down the long line a silent call is thrilled;
Ten thousand buds to moonlit glory flower;
Then thousand star-white blooms
with light are filled.

from "Night-Blooming Cereus" by Don Blanding

Night-Blooming Cereus

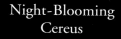

This climbing cactus has
an ordinary appearance
for most of the year. But
for a brief period each
summer—especially
during the months of
July and August—it
bursts into bloom after
dark, each spectacular
white and yellow
blossom lasting for a
single night only.

Lono [god of planting and harvests]
. . . decreed [to proclaim the start of
the annual celebration of Makahiki]
that man was forbidden to kill; war
was prohibited, there was to be no
fighting; the ocean was kapu, *not a*
canoe was to sail; the kapa *anvil was*
kapu, *and no cloth was to be beaten;*
the drum was kapu, *not to be tapped;*
the conch shell was kapu, *not to be*
blown; the land was kapu *to Lono,*
the earth, life, the mountain, the
ocean, the raging surf, the family,
the sailing canoe was kapu *to Lono.*

from *Fornander Collection of*
Hawaiian Antiquities and Folk-Lore

Kauila

Kauila is an endemic
tree, now rare. The
Hawaiians used its
extremely hard wood
to fashion spears, tapa
beaters, and tools for
digging and cultivating
the land. The staff that
the god Kāne thrust into
the rock to bring forth
water when he and
Kanaloa were in the
uplands of East Maui
was made of kauila
wood. And the long
staff that symbolized
the god Lono and was
carried at the head of
the annual Makahiki
procession was also
made of kauila.

E kau mai ana ka hali'a
No sweet tubarose poina 'ole

Me he ala e 'i mai ana ia'u
He welina pau 'ole me ia pua

Aloha ku'u pua ala onaona
I wili 'ia me maile lauli'i

Ke hea nei ku'u lei 'ala onaona
E ho'i mai kāua la e pili

Ha'ina 'ia mai ana ka puana
Ku'u pua tubarose poina 'ole

A fond memory comes to me
Of the sweet tuberose, so unforgettable

Like fragrance, it speaks to me
Forever greeting this flower with affection

Love for this sweet fragrant flower
Entwined with small leaf maile

Where is this lei of mine, so fragrant?
Return and let us be together

The story is told
Of my unforgettable sweet tuberose

lyrics to "Pua Tubarose" by Kimo Kamana

Tuberose

*The tuberose is
a native of Mexico,
now grown widely in
the islands. With their
exquisitely delicate
beauty and seductive,
nearly intoxicating
fragrance, the flowers—
often "entwined with
small leaf maile"—
remain a popular
choice for leis.*

*The wildwoods of Hawaii furnished
in great abundance and variety . . .
sweet-scented leaves and flowers suitable
for its [the hula-hall altar's] decoration.
A spirit of fitness, however, limited
choice among these to certain species that
were deemed acceptable to the goddess
[Laka, goddess of the hula] because they
were reckoned as among her favorite
forms of metamorphosis. To go outside
this ordained and traditional range
would have been an offense, a sacrilege.
This critical spirit would have looked
with the greatest disfavor on the practice
that in modern times has crept in, of
bedecking the dancers with garlands of
roses, pinks, jessamine, and other non-
indigenous flowers, as being utterly repug-
nant to the traditional spirit of the hula.*

from *Unwritten Literature of Hawaii:
The Sacred Songs of the Hula*
by Nathaniel B. Emerson

'Ōhiʻa Lehua

*Sacred to Pele, the
goddess of volcanoes, the
'ōhiʻa lehua (opposite,
inset, and in silhouette),
was also considered an
embodiment of Laka,
one of the goddesses of
the hula; as such, it was
another of the plants
placed as offerings on the
altar of the hula hālau.
It is the official flower of
the island of Hawaiʻi.*

The white flowers below my window
resemble naupaka, but are not.
At night, ghosts, but not. When your envelope
arrived with missing hands and sealed
mouth, I thought another woman.
You must have shown her the naupaka—
one half stranded in the sand,
the other on the mountain.
It's always the same story with flowers.

"White Eclipse" by Lisa Erb

Mountain Naupaka

According to a Hawaiian
legend, two lovers were
separated; one became
the mountain naupaka
(naupaka kuahiwi); *the*
other, beach naupaka
(naupaka kahakai).
That is why the flowers
of each plant appear to
have been cut in half.
Of the several species of
naupaka found in the
islands, all are endemic
except for the beach
naupaka, which
is indigenous.

You thrive in the mountains
appearing but half-fulfilled.
Unsettled at the beach I remain
split down the middle.
Remember when we blossomed as one?
The legend was never a myth
for presently you're drinking rain
in a distant valley
and I, my roots, dig deeper
far below the parched sand
and we're near each other
only when we remember
this story of the naupaka flower.

"We Both Remember" by Richard Hamasaki

Beach Naupaka

The beach naupaka
(naupaka kahakai)
was, according to one
Hawaiian chant, born
of heaven and earth.
Its white berries have
given rise to another
Hawaiian name for
the plant: huahekili,
"hailstones."

*Without an exception the men and women wore
wreaths and garlands of flowers, carmine, orange,
or pure white, twined round their hats, and
thrown carelessly round their necks, flowers
unknown to me, but redolent of the tropics in
fragrance and colour. Many of the young beauties
wore the gorgeous blossom of the red hibiscus
among their abundant, unconfined, black hair,
and many, besides the garlands, wore festoons
of a sweet-scented vine, or of an exquisitely
beautiful fern, knotted behind and hanging
half-way down their dresses. These adornments
of natural flowers are most attractive.*

from *Six Months in the Sandwich Islands* by Isabella Bird

Spider Lily

*Introduced to Hawaiʻi
from tropical America,
the spider lily, with its
fragrant flowers, was
a favorite of Queen
Emma's. It is a member
of the amaryllis family,
as are the tuberose,
narcissus, century plant,
and sisal, among
many others.*

Lau ʻōlena lau pālulu
E peʻe nei kau mōhala
O ka makani hāwanawana
Hōʻike nei pua ʻōlena
I kou nani
Pua ʻōlena, pua ʻōlena

Leaf ʻōlena, leaf that shelters
  and protects
Hiding the blossom unfolding
The wind whispers
See here the ʻōlena blossom
Show your beauty
ʻŌlena blossom, ʻōlena blossom

lyrics from "Pua ʻŌlena"
by Jimmy Kaholokula

102

ʻŌlena

*Once found
in abundance in
Hawaiʻi's forests,
ʻōlena is now rare in
the islands. Its leaves
rise directly from under-
ground stems, supporting
a flower cluster at their
center. The plant,
known in English as
turmeric, is widely used
as a spice. The early
Hawaiians incorporated
it in certain purification
ceremonies, also using
the root medicinally
and to make a dye
for tapa.*

This good world of Maui lying spread out before him, he saw, was not a place of beauty. And yet neither was it a place of ugliness. It was stark and raw. It was brutal and untamed. . . .

And yet he knew it was not as empty as it appeared to be. Even in that seeming desert certain small plants grew, some tiny animals crept. And wherever on Maui's hard body water lingered life could be found in abundance. Along the banks of the river flowing past his feet, in the high-walled valley from which it came, many kinds of trees, ferns, and grasses thrived. Around the edges of the swamp near Kahului, and on the northern shoulder of Haleakala, where clouds gathered and dropped their rain, the green of life sprang up, to show that the earth beneath [was] good.

from *The Stone of Kannon* by O. A. Bushnell

Aphelandra Aurantiaca

Also known as "fiery spike," Aphelandra aurantiaca *is an herb that originated in Mexico and other parts of tropical America. It is a member of the acanthus family. Its tiny but brilliant flowers can indeed provide a fiery sparkle amid the ground cover of even the darkest rainforest areas.*

The naio *. . . is a sweet-scented*
wood and of great hardness.

from *Hawaiian Antiquities*
(Moolelo Hawaii) by David Malo

Naio

At one time naio *was*
to be found on all of
Hawai'i's main islands,
especially in coastal
areas. Its durable wood
was used for support
posts in the construction
of thatched houses.
Naio *is also known*
as false sandalwood,
owing to the fact that
its heartwood has a
similar spicy aroma.

A million moons over Hawaii
A million tunes to lullabye me
An endless garden paradise is mine
Where ev'ry flower reveals your face divine

lyrics from "A Million Moons over Hawaii"
by Billy Abrams and Andy Alone Long

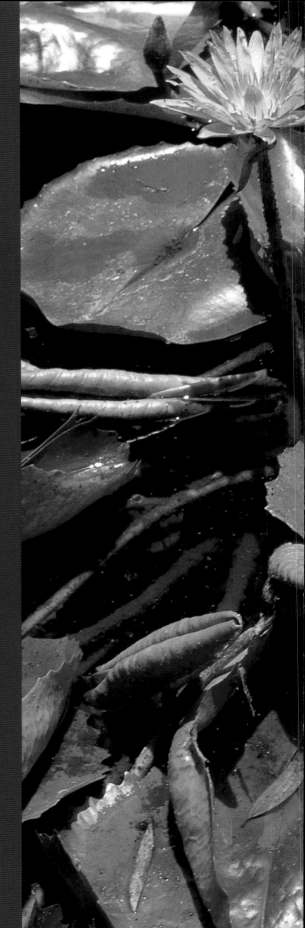

Waterlily

*Though many species
of waterlilies originated
in tropical climes, none
is native to Hawai'i.
Related to the lotus, the
waterlily was considered
sacred in ancient Egypt,
as is the lotus in many
Asian cultures. Some
botanists believe that
both may be descendants
of the earth's earliest
flowering plants. Fossil
waterlily seeds have been
found that date back to
the late Mesozoic Era,
around the time of
the disappearance of
the dinosaurs.*

. . . Can you
Look through my eyes and see this land
Where beauty lives on every hand?
· . . . I'll give
My heart to you so you may live
One day in Paradise. . . .

from "Leaves from My Grass-House"
by Don Blanding

110

Bromeliad

Bromeliads are part
of the pineapple family,
all members of which
originated in tropical
or subtropical America.
Many bromeliad species
have been introduced
to Hawai'i, two of
which are shown
here: the portea *(left),*
from Brazil, and the
aechmea *(opposite).*

A Wai-akea, i ka Hilo-hana-kahi,
Ala i ka wa po iki,
I ka lehua lei o Hilo, o Hi-lo;
E pauku ana no ka hala me ka lehua.
Maikai Hilo, o Hilo-hana-kahi!

At Wai-akea, in Hilo—
The Hilo of Hana-kahi—
They rise in the early morning
To weave fresh wreaths of lehua,
Inbeading its bloom with hala—
Gay Hilo of Hana-kahi!

from *Pele and Hiiaka: A Myth from Hawaii*
by Nathaniel B. Emerson

112

Hala

Hala *is indigenous to*
Hawai'i, other Pacific
islands, and parts of
southern Asia. In English
it is called pandanus or
screw pine. It is related
to the endemic 'ie'ie *vine.*
Aerial roots support the
trunk above the ground.
The Hawaiians plaited
hala *leaves, or* lau hala,
for a variety of uses,
including canoe sails,
fans, mats for the floor
and for sleeping, baskets,
and sometimes even
house thatching.

That night, Taizo came home in
his casket. He lay in the parlor near
the altar. . . . I crept to my brother
only when alone. What surprised me
most was how easily death had come,
for until then I had assumed death
was more than a childhood struggle. . . .

People left flowers in our parlor and
outside our front door. I pulled the bud
from a ginger plant and took it to my
room. That night I unwrapped a
layer from the bud and made a whistle.
I lay in bed and whistled carefully,
quietly, remembering how recklessly
my brother and I had whistled with
our mouths toward the sky.

from *Middle Son* by Deborah Iida

Red Ginger

Another member of
the large ginger family,
this lovely plant, whose
scientific name is alpinia
purpurata, *is a native*
of the south Pacific. Its
name in Hawaiian is
ʻawapuhi ʻulaʻula. *It*
is commonly used as an
ornamental in Hawaiʻi.
A pleasant fragrance is
released when the roots
or stems are cut.

Kāua i ka one o Maniniholo,
Tuʻu ipo i ke kai holu o Makua.
Ulu hala o Naue kaʻu aloha,
I ka nou hala ʻole a ka Lūpua.
Onaona nā lehua o Luluʻupali,
Noho ana i ka poli a Kaʻumaka.
Haʻina ʻia mai ka puana
Tuʻu ipo i ke kai holu o Makua.

Let us go to the sand of Maniniholo,
O sweetheart of the swaying sea of Makua.
For the hala *grove of Naue is my love,*
Ever pelted by the Lūpua breeze.
Sweet are the lehua *of Luluʻupali,*
That sit near the bosom of Kaʻumaka.
This is the end of my song,
My sweetheart of the swaying sea of Makua.

from "Aia i Niʻihau Kuʻu Pāwehe"

Pōhinahina

Known in English as
beach vitex, pōhinahina
is an indigenous shrub
of the verbena family
and, as such, is related
to teak. It may be found
growing wild along
Hawaiʻi's shores and
as far away as India
and Japan.

There is a melody
Forever haunting me
A thousand times retold
A theme that's never old

There's the perfume of a million flowers
Clinging to the heart of old Hawaii
There's a rainbow following the showers
Bringing me a part of old Hawaii

There's a silver moon
A symphony of stars
There's a hula tune
And the hum of soft guitars

There's the tradewind
Sighing in the heavens
Singing me
A song of old Hawaii

lyrics from "A Song of Old Hawaii"
by Gordon Beecher and Johnny Noble

118

Ixora

*Ixora plants are
members of the coffee
family. The several
species come from many
parts of the world—
Madagascar, China,
India, and elsewhere.
The name derives from
the Hindu god Iswara,
to whom the flowers
were given as offerings.
The species shown here
is known in Hawai'i
as* pōpōlehua.

To hear the mornings
   among hāpuʻu: *a purity*
of cardinals, cunning bees
   in shell-covered sleeves
     of honeysuckle,
         . . . *the aqua undertones*
   of cooing doves.

To seek our scarlet
   ʻapapane, *Hōpoe restless*
     amongst the liko
       and ʻōlapa *trees,*
   shimmering the leaves,
     . . . shush-shush
       of burnt rain
         sweeping in from Puna.

To watch our lustrous
   volcanic dawn seducing
     ʻelepaio, *speckled beak*
   sucking ʻōhelo *berries*
     oozing sap
       under a crimson sun.

To breathe the Akua:
   lehua *and* makani,
     pua *and* lāʻī,
       maile *and* palai,
         . . . *pungent* kino lau.

To sense the ancients,
     ka wā mamua—*from time before*
   slumbering still
     amidst the forests
       of Kaʻū, within the bosom
         of Pele.

To honor and chant,
   by the sound
     of the pū, *our*
   ageless genealogy:
ʻāina aloha,
   ʻāina hānau,
     . . . *this generous, native Hawaiʻi.*

"To Hear the Mornings"
by Haunani-Kay Trask

ʻAlaʻalawainui

This small succulent
is a native herb found,
often in forests, on all
of the islands, but
mainly on Oʻahu and
Hawaiʻi. Like ʻawa,
to which it is related,
it is a member of the
black pepper family.
The Hawaiians made
a gray dye for tapa
from its ashes.

At cold daybreak
we wind
up the mountainside
to Haleakala Crater.
Our hands knot
under the rough of
your old army blanket.

We pass protea
and carnation farms
in Kula,
drive through
desolate rockfields.

Upon this one place
on Earth,
from the ancient
lava rivers,
silverswords rise,
startled
into starbursts
by the sun.
Like love, sometimes,
they die
at their first
and rare flowering.

"Silverswords"
by Juliet S. Kono

Silversword

The native silversword,
ʻāhinahina in Hawaiian,
is found only in the
crater of Haleakalā,
East Maui, at elevations
above 6,000 feet. An
individual plant may
grow for some fifty
years in its compact,
"starburst" form before a
stalk bearing a hundred
or more flower heads
emerges, reaching its full
development in a matter
of weeks. After it flowers,
the plant dies.

selected bibliography

Abbott, Isabella Aiona. *Lā'au Hawai'i: Traditional Hawaiian Uses of Plants.* Honolulu: Bishop Museum Press, 1992.

Beckwith, Martha. *Hawaiian Mythology.* New Haven: Yale University Press, 1940. Reprint, with an introduction by Katharine Luomala, Honolulu: University of Hawaii Press, 1970.

————, trans. and ed. *The Kumulipo: A Hawaiian Creation Chant.* Chicago: University of Chicago Press, 1951. Reprint, Honolulu: University of Hawaii Press, 1972.

Bird, Isabella L. *Six Months in the Sandwich Islands.* London: John Murray, 1875. Reprint, Honolulu: University of Hawaii Press for Friends of the Library of Hawaii, 1964.

Blanding, Don. *Vagabond's House.* New York: Dodd, Mead, 1928.

Bushnell, O. A. *Ka'a'awa: A Novel about Hawai'i in the 1850s.* Honolulu: University of Hawaii Press, 1972.

————. *The Stone of Kannon.* Honolulu: University of Hawaii Press for Friends of the Library of Hawaii, 1979.

Chock, Eric, James R. Harstad, Darrell H. Y. Lum and Bill Teter, eds. *Growing up Local: An Anthology of Poetry and Prose from Hawai'i.* Honolulu: Bamboo Ridge Press, 1998.

Chock, Eric, and Darrell H. Y. Lum, eds. *Paké: Writings by Chinese in Hawai'i.* Honolulu: Bamboo Ridge Press, 1989.

Daws, Gavan. *Shoal of Time: A History of the Hawaiian Islands.* Honolulu: University of Hawaii Press, 1968.

Elbert, Samuel H., ed. *Selections from Fornander's Hawaiian Antiquities and Folk-Lore.* Honolulu: University of Hawaii Press, 1959.

Elbert, Samuel H., and Noelani K. Mahoe. *Nā Mele o Hawai'i Nei: 101 Hawaiian Songs.* Honolulu: University of Hawaii Press, 1970.

Emerson, Nathaniel B. *Pele and Hiiaka: A Myth from Hawaii.* Honolulu: Honolulu Star-Bulletin, Ltd., 1915. Reprint, Honolulu: 'Ai Pōhaku Press, 1993.

————. *Unwritten Literature of Hawai'i: The Sacred Songs of the Hula.* Washington, D.C.: Bureau of American Ethnology, 1909. Reprint, Rutland, Vt., and Tokyo: Charles E. Tuttle, 1965.

Gay, Lawrence Kainoahou. *True Stories of the Island of Lanai.* Honolulu: [self-published], 1965.

Hamasaki, Richard. *From the Spider Bone Diaries: Poems and Songs.* Honolulu: University of Hawai'i Press, 2002.

Handy, E. S. Craighill, Kenneth P. Emory, Edwin H. Bryan, Peter H. Buck, John H. Wise, and others. *Ancient Hawaiian Civilization.* Rev. ed. Rutland, Vt., and Tokyo: Charles E. Tuttle, 1965.

Handy, E. S. Craighill, and Elizabeth Green Handy. *Native Planters in Old Hawaii: Their Life, Lore, and Environment.* With the collaboration of Mary Kawena Pukui. Rev. ed. Honolulu: Bishop Museum Press, 1991.

Harstad, Cheryl A. and James R. Harstad, eds. *Island Fire: An Anthology of Literature from Hawai'i.* Honolulu: Curriculum Research & Development Group and University of Hawai'i Press, 2002.

Iida, Deborah. *Middle Son.* Chapel Hill, N.C.: Algonquin Books, 1996.

Juvik, Sonia P., and James O. Juvik, eds. *Atlas of Hawai'i.* 3d ed. Honolulu: University of Hawai'i Press, 1998.

Kamakau, Samuel Manaiakalani. *Ka Po'e Kahiko: The People of Old.* Translated from the newspaper Ke Au 'Oko'a by Mary Kawena Pukui, arranged and edited by Dorothy B. Barrère. 1964. Reprint, Honolulu: Bishop Museum Press, 1991.

———. *The Works of the People of Old: Nā Hana a ka Po'e Kahiko.* Translated from the newspaper Ke Au 'Oko'a by Mary Kawena Pukui, arranged and edited by Dorothy B. Barrère. Honolulu: Bishop Museum Press, 1976.

Kauhi, Emma Kapūohu'ulaokalani. *Story of Kapa'ahu: He Mo'olelo no Kapa'ahu.* Translated by Charles M. Langlas. Kapa'ahu, Puna: [self-published], 1996.

Kawajo, Yutaka. *Who da Guy?* Honolulu: Sparky Press, 2000.

Keller, Nora Okja, Brenda Kwon, Sun Namkung, Gary Pak, and Cathy Song, eds. *Yobo: Korean American Writing in Hawai'i.* Honolulu: Bamboo Ridge Press, 2003.

Kepler, Angela Kay. *Hawai'i's Floral Splendor.* Honolulu: Mutual Publishing, 1997.

Kirch, Patrick Vinton. *Feathered Gods and Fishhooks: An Introduction to Hawaiian Archaeology and Prehistory.* Honolulu: University of Hawaii Press, 1985.

Kono, Juliet S. *Hilo Rains.* Honolulu: Bamboo Ridge Press, 1988.

Kono, Juliet S., and Cathy Song, eds. *Sister Stew: Fiction and Poetry by Women.* Honolulu: Bamboo Ridge Press, 1991.

Lodge, David. *Paradise News, A Novel.* New York: Penguin Books, 1991.

125

Malo, David. *Hawaiian Antiquities (Moolelo Hawaii)*. Translated from the Hawaiian by Dr. Nathaniel B. Emerson. Honolulu: Hawaiian Gazette Co., Ltd, 1903. 2d ed. Honolulu: Bishop Museum Press, 1951.

Merwin, W. S. *The Folding Cliffs: A Narrative*. New York: Knopf, 1998.

Mitchell, Donald D. Kilolani. *Resource Units in Hawaiian Culture*. Rev. ed. Honolulu: The Kamehameha Schools Press, 1982.

Murayama, Milton. *Five Years on a Rock*. Honolulu: University of Hawaii Press, 1994.

Neal, Marie C. *In Gardens of Hawaii*. Honolulu: Bishop Museum Press, 1965.

Pitchford, Genie. *Hawaiian Time*. Designs by Stanley Stubenberg. Honolulu: Watkins & Sturgis, Ltd., 1955.

Porteus, Stanley D. *Calabashes and Kings: An Introduction to Hawaii*. Palo Alto, Calif.: Pacific Books, 1945.

Pukui, Mary Kawena, and Alfons L. Korn, eds. and trans. *The Echo of Our Song: Chants & Poems of the Hawaiians*. Honolulu: University of Hawaii Press, 1973.

Pukui, Mary Kawena, and Samuel H. Elbert. *Hawaiian Dictionary*. Rev. and enl. ed. Honolulu: University of Hawaii Press, 1986.

Pukui, Mary Kawena, coll. and trans. *Folktales of Hawai'i: He Mau Ka'ao Hawai'i*. With Laura C. S. Green. Honolulu: Bishop Museum Press, 1995.

————, trans. *Nā Mele Welo: Songs of Our Heritage*. Arranged and edited by Pat Namaka Bacon and Nathan Napoka. Honolulu: Bishop Museum Press, 1995.

Salvador, Normie. "Spiders in the Field: A Young Filipino Writer in Hawai'i." *Hybolics* 3 (2002): 10–11.

Stanton, Joseph, ed. *A Hawai'i Anthology: A Collection of Works by Recipients of the Hawai'i Award for Literature, 1974–1996*. Honolulu: State Foundation on Culture and the Arts, 1997.

Stevenson, Robert Louis. *Travels in Hawaii*. Edited and with an introduction by A. Grove Day. Honolulu: University of Hawaii Press, 1973.

Trask, Haunani-Kay. *Light in the Crevice Never Seen*. Rev. ed. Corvallis, Ore.: Calyx Books, 1999.

————. *Night Is a Sharkskin Drum*. Honolulu: University of Hawai'i Press, 2002.

Tyau, Kathleen. *Makai*. Boston: Beacon Press, 1999.

acknowledgments

WE ARE INDEBTED to those whose names appear in the bibliography, particularly to Isabella Aiona Abbott, E. S. Craighill Handy and his collaborators, and Marie C. Neal, whose research and writings are the sources of much of the factual information related to plants that appears in the introduction to this book and in the captions accompanying the photographs. Our main endeavor in this regard has been simply to gather, cull, and distill information that is available in the several important studies that they, and others, have published. We are grateful to the many writers and publishers who have graciously consented to let us reprint excerpts from their works, the details of which appear in the Credits that follow, on page 128.

We would like to express our sincere gratitude to Isabella Abbott for reviewing the botanical information and suggesting revisions. Any mistakes that may remain are of course our responsibility. We would also like to extend a special thank you to Carol Silva for her careful review of the introduction before publication. Our thanks go out as well to the following individuals for generous advice or other assistance while the book was in preparation:

Kula Abiva, Watermark Publishing; Frederika Bain; Gerald D. Carr, Botany Department, University of Hawai'i at Mānoa; Lopaka Kapanui; Wendy Kim Messier; Maile Meyer and Elena Shinagawa of Native Books/Nā Mea Hawai'i; Joy K. Nakagawa; Diane Ragone, National Tropical Botanical Garden, Kaua'i; Cheryl Sherman, who pointed us in Watermark's direction; Robinson Wageman, our son and hiking companion; Judy and Katsuo Yasutake; Sarah Yasutake, our daughter and discerning editor; the staff at Lyon Arboretum, O'ahu, particularly Ray Baker, Liz Huppman, and Karen Shigematsu, for invaluable help in unraveling or verifying several plant identifications; and the staff and rangers of the National Park Service at Haleakalā National Park, Maui. Finally, our thanks to George Engebretson and Leo Gonzalez of Watermark Publishing for their interest in this project.

credits